Weather Your Storm

Watching Irma barnstorm through South Florida from a gap between the kitchen window shutters, September, 2017

SHERNA SPENCER

Book Series: Living Lively

An imprint of **SGS Publishing**
www.LookItsTheBook.com

Weather Your Storm
Copyright @2018, by Sherna G. Spencer. All rights reserved. Except as permitted under the U.S. Copyright Act of 1976, no part of this publication may be reproduced, distributed, or transmitted in any form or by any means, or stored in a database or retrieval system, without the prior written permission of the publisher.

Published by JALOUSIE, an imprint of SGS Publishing, LLC
4500 W. Oakland Park Boulevard, Ste 103
Fort Lauderdale, FL 33313

Cover Design: Beresford Nicholson

Weather Your Storm is a work of fiction. Names, characters, places, and incidents are the product of the author's imagination or are used fictionally. Any resemblance to actual events, locales, or persons, living or dead, is coincidental.

Publisher's Cataloging-in-Publication data
Spencer, Sherna G
      Weather Your Storm
      p.cm
      ISBN: 978-0-9997270-2-7
      ISBN for eBook: 978-0-9997270-3-4
1. Self-Help - Journaling 2. Self-Help – Motivational & Inspirational 3. Self-Help - Personal Growth and Happiness 4.Title-

Library of Congress Control number LCN: LLCN: 2017919118

First Edition: April 2018   SCANNABLE

Printed in the United States of America

Quantity Discounts are available. Contact the publisher
      www.lookitsthebook.com
      talk@lookitsthebook.com
      954-714-8123

Watching Irma and Feeling Her Effects

Contents

Past Perfect, Present Tense 11
Outside In 13
No Chicken 15
Layers 17
Making A Connection 19
Certainty 21
Lashing 23
Cool Down 25
Thy Will 27
On Shore 29
Tighten The Screw, Then Release 31
Irma: You are Just A Pain 33
The First Available Shore 35
Four Things I Learned From Irma 37

Table of Contents story
TOC story ™

During Irma, I went through a lot - I waited until she finished Lashing us and when she was Cooling Down, I made my move. I was No Chicken. I went through many Layers, but I was determined to Make a Connection. At that time I was thinking that it was Thy Will, for my Past seemed Perfect, compared what I was going through in those Present moments, which was Tense. I told myself that I would have to be brave, Tighten the Screw and when it is over, I would just Release it. With Certainty, I can say that Irma was Just A Pain but I at least Learned Four Things from my experience meeting her. Thankfully I was not Outside but In, when we met.

Phew. It's over. I am On the Shore finally. I took the first one I saw as I came out of my storm, it was the First Available one.

Past Perfect, Present Tense

We have our past.
It is what we know.
We can see what settled where,
after our storm

We have our recollection.
It is what we wondered about.
The when, where, who, what and why,
during our storm

We have now.
In the present. It's tense
since the when, where, who, what and why
is still unfolding

7:00 AM *on* **Thursday, September 7**: *Wanting to jump on a plane, a train, boat or anything that moves, so I can leave Florida, but it is too late, everything is shut down. We cannot drive, it is a parking lot on the highways going north. Sigh. So plan B; Batten down and ride it out, praying.*

UPDATE: 4:13 AM *on* **Saturday, September 9**: *Listening to the radio, waiting on Irma. A lady was speaking. She was from one of the Caribbean islands that Irma had stormed through before coming to South Florida. She was saying that all they had left was each other. Everything else was gone, she said and added "all of us are in the same boat, none can help the other, we do not know when things will change or how."*

Outside In

Salvador Dali's heir no more.
Ah, but she was so sure.
He was exhumed
and plumed
by her information,
but the doctors presented their own revelation.
Her DNA was not wound in Dali.
Ah, so close.
An almost Svengali?

Am I who I am because of who I say I am or
am I who I am because of who knows me?
Am I still who I am if no one knows who I am?
Can I be who I am if no one knows me?
Who am I if no one knows me?
Will I be someone else if no one else knows who I am?

3:20 PM *on* **Saturday, September 9**: *Preparing for Irma's arrival.*

No Chicken

An impetuous youngster or a
marauding monster,
bounding
seeking
play or
prey.

We're under the gun,
frozen,
stoic,
waiting
for her energy to
run its course

5:22 PM *on* **Saturday, September 9:** *Still preparing and waiting for Irma.*

Layers

The lime green curtain fabric, it's see-through; it has vertical lines which are dotted exactly every two inches, with a green thread bunched on top of the line, in the shape of a fern. It takes my spirits outside.

So too the rumble of thunder echoing every so often. It is extending its baritone (sometimes popping my ear drums) on which the wind rolls itself out, around the earth's floor.

12:24 PM *on* **Sunday, September 10:** *Irma is doing what she wants to do. She is coming slowly. It is like putting your toes in to test the water before going in and fully submerging yourself.*

Making A Connection

Tentacles of ice, bolts of lightening, electric lines, the
internet; inlets running into the sea.
An eclectic bunch,
but none are self-contained.
All are seekers
searching to find a mate,
a home
where they connect with another part of themselves.

1:33 PM *on* **Sunday, September 10:** *Irma does her touch and go. She is taking practice shots on South Florida and doing very well.*

Certainty

How much uncertainty can one withstand?
With what can one shore up his grit?
Can it be done through practice
(like training to firm up your biceps or to flatten your tummy)?
If so, sign me up for the class.

I fear my uncertainty is now as a wineglass
susceptible of being smashed
with the mere nick of a straw
to leave me shattered,
in pieces
that will be bouncing and skating willy-nilly across the cold
hard
sun bright tile,
before settling down
to adorn them with translucent crystals.

3:16 PM *on* **Sunday, September 10**: *Irma is in high spirits as though she has just taken another full glass of wine, while my head feels that I too have overindulged. Just noticing that the canal is much higher than normal and the water has gone from walk-in-the-park placid to speed dating, fast moving and unpredictable.*

Lashing

It's not fun…not like a wet towel on the beach for play
She is showing us she's in charge today,
lashing fine lines of rain out and all about - take this and that -
but the wind deflects her most ardent supporters.

Pacing back and forth in the living room, arms on my waist.
"Oh no, it's finally becoming like Andrew…."
"Take it easy Mom, go write a poem or something, read your bible…"

I peep through a space between the hurricane shutters.
"The canal is rising, take up everything off the floor, one strong surge and that is it."
"Mom it will have to come over the embankment first."
"Just help me with this rug and take all the boxes and put them on chairs."
She shrugs and complies then retreats to her cave.
The trees weep, laden with their burden, nowhere to run, nowhere to hide.
They take it
and take it
and take it
and take it some more.
They bear it all
and not with a grin

4:07 PM *on* **Sunday, September 10**: *Irma is not joking, but who is really in charge? I am standing, writing this and wondering when the canal will climb into my living room and how long the lights will last.*

Cool Down

In the words of the "cool ruler" Gregory Isaacs,
"Irma, cool down the pace for me little woman, you rocking it too fast for me..."
"Just cool down, cool down, cool down, cool down, cool down.
Not so fast."

Calm Down Irma, cool it down, stop chasing Harvey.
He's too fast for you.

You don't have to keep up with the boys
set your own standard lady.
We know you are up to it.
We hear you
we feel you
let it out
let it go
let it go.
Just let him go

4:17 PM *on* **Sunday, September 10**: *Irma continues to show her force. I am now talking to her, trying to let her know I have been there, trying to soothe her, woman to woman.*

Thy Will

Be done on South Florida, Irma.
Be done.

Let's see the **A**nts and the antelope
the **B**irds, bumble bees
the **C**hildren playing hide and seek
the **D**awn peeping through misty folds of the darkness and
the deer dashing home
the **E**ggs being born amidst the chatter in the coop
the **F**lorida sun (even in September) and the fish fries
(with the accompanying festival)
the **G**oats, bearded - black, white, brown – why do they
always seem to have a frown
Holy men and women, Gentiles, Jews, and in between, all
on their knees, in one accord – making supplications to
our maker;
Insects running for shade and indigo, yellow and
aquamarine – all color palates blooming and I am aspiring
for insight and irie. I am itching to savor
the **J**une plum's tartness and sweet as it hits the taste buds
in my jaw; I'll be jumping, jumping at J'ouvert, and we'll be
jumping for joy, jumping with the children, now danger's
past and
Keeping time as an afterthought;
Looking around outside
Moving from here to there,
a **N**ew bud to plant, it's a new day, cleansed for the new
beginning, a new boldness with blessings by
One love, One God, on
Purpose, populating the land, people feel it – it will now spark

Questions without answers (the believers cede), but in time they will be revealed.
Reasonable women and men were assured dominion above all, so
Stand tall even with nothing at all (but the goodness of Jah in your pocket), stride
Towards the new day, turn over a new leaf on your life, take a chance, work in
Unison, U.N.I.T.Y., the chain is stronger than each link
Verily (victoriously) a promise was made just as the moon, the stars and sun
Was made for your purpose
Xhale. There is more, we are more than our body's constraints, we are Xtra (not ordinary)
Yellows, Yawehs, Yeshivas and yonder throngs are the onlookers praying for our deliverance and a
Zen experience

2:33 AM on Monday, September 11: *She's gone! Good riddance. I'm a little hyped up. Goodnight and goodbye, Irma!*

On Shore

At dawn, they found me washed up on the sea shore.
A whale had belched me out whole.
Its teeth were blunted and could not gnaw on the spirit
that encircled me.
I laid there shivering.
My mouth opened and fish, leaves and sea water drained
from the bowels of my body.
They poured clear, fresh water over me.
Bits of black and gray scales blew off in all directions.
When the water finally hit my skin, it felt like fire igniting
each pore on my body.
Gradually it cooled me.
They wrapped me in soft cloths.
Eyes forced my lashes apart and I looked up and saw a
grey sky standing guard.
Then a bright white light with brilliant diamond rays
pushed through.
I basked in its brilliance
and its army of energy jets injected my veins with vitality.
'twas a rebirth
a morning
a good morning
in Zion

7:50 AM *on* **Monday, September 11**: *It's over. Proper sleep is needed.*

Tighten The Screw, Then Release

Each time a slap or an arrow landed, the screw tightened,
shuttering your goals.
Desolation descends.
Release it.
Sit on the floor.
Take deep breaths.
Close eyes tightly till they hurt.
Pray.
Stand up.
Put one foot in front of the other.
Walk on out.
Look ahead.
Sing.
Smile.
Keep going.
It will be better soon.

Tuesday, September 12: *At home, we have life.*

Irma: You are Just A Pain

I don't have to strain
to remember
how
I got this sprain.

Irma, you hit terra firma and
bounced about
running after that lout
Harvey.

You caused a strain on our
nerves and our
reserves.

You are gone, but not
in memory
You linger on my
big finger.

Saturday, September 16: *You were such a pain Irma. You hurt.*

The First Available Shore

You were on your way
somewhere
You were plodding or steaming
along.
Then a storm roused itself

When you are out at sea
and an Irma comes
on the scene,
change direction.
Reset your goal

Look for and
pull into the first available port, the
first available place to shelter,
so you can ride out the storm
safely

Meditate and
pray for heavenly guidance to the location of that
safe harbor and
change your direction towards it.
Go there and
pull in

A few days later: *Listening to the radio as persons call in to talk about their Florida Irma experience. A lady said that she was surprised at the reaction of her neighbors. She said that before Irma arrived they all were friendly and pledged to help each other regardless of what happened. She said* *that as soon as Irma passed and there was no great damage for anyone of them, they all turned on their generators and closed their doors. She had to beg one of them for cool water – for her dogs she said because she lives alone and she does not have a generator; of course her neighbors know that.*

QUESTION: *After a near catastrophe do we retreat to who we were, or is there a part of us that will forever relive the touch of panic and know that we are not invincible.*

Four Things I Learned From Irma

1. prepare for the unknown - meditation or prayer
2. don't stay alone. When you are going through a storm, you need company
3. safeguard your important papers or treasures (what you can carry away quickly if needs be, in a backpack)
4. life is tenuous - a second can change things for the worse – make your life have an impact by contributing to the life of someone else

About the Author

SHERNA SPENCER's roots spring from the island of Jamaica. Her love of books and language began there in a Parish library in Manchester. After moving to the U.S, she attended Le Moyne College in upstate New York. There, she obtained a Bachelors degree, with dual majors in English and Spanish. She continued her studies in Italy and thereafter completed her law degree at the University of Miami School of Law. She is currently an attorney in Fort Lauderdale, Florida where she was the host of a radio program about immigration and nationality law, for 9 years.

Other Books By The Author

Musing Aloud, Allowed
Three Echoes Dancing
It's the Context
30 Ways to Lift Your Spirits, Not Your Eyebrows

WEATHER YOUR STORM

WEATHER YOUR STORM

WEATHER YOUR STORM

WEATHER YOUR STORM

WEATHER YOUR STORM

WEATHER YOUR STORM

WEATHER YOUR STORM

WEATHER YOUR STORM

WEATHER YOUR STORM

WEATHER YOUR STORM

WEATHER YOUR STORM

WEATHER YOUR STORM

WEATHER YOUR STORM

WEATHER YOUR STORM

WEATHER YOUR STORM

WEATHER YOUR STORM

WEATHER YOUR STORM

WEATHER YOUR STORM

WEATHER YOUR STORM

WEATHER YOUR STORM

WEATHER YOUR STORM

WEATHER YOUR STORM

WEATHER YOUR STORM

WEATHER YOUR STORM

WEATHER YOUR STORM

WEATHER YOUR STORM

WEATHER YOUR STORM

WEATHER YOUR STORM

WEATHER YOUR STORM

WEATHER YOUR STORM

WEATHER YOUR STORM

WEATHER YOUR STORM

WEATHER YOUR STORM

WEATHER YOUR STORM

WEATHER YOUR STORM

WEATHER YOUR STORM

WEATHER YOUR STORM

WEATHER YOUR STORM

WEATHER YOUR STORM

WEATHER YOUR STORM

WEATHER YOUR STORM

WEATHER YOUR STORM

WEATHER YOUR STORM

WEATHER YOUR STORM

WEATHER YOUR STORM

WEATHER YOUR STORM

WEATHER YOUR STORM

WEATHER YOUR STORM

WEATHER YOUR STORM

WEATHER YOUR STORM

WEATHER YOUR STORM

WEATHER YOUR STORM

WEATHER YOUR STORM

WEATHER YOUR STORM

WEATHER YOUR STORM

WEATHER YOUR STORM

WEATHER YOUR STORM

WEATHER YOUR STORM

WEATHER YOUR STORM

WEATHER YOUR STORM

WEATHER YOUR STORM

WEATHER YOUR STORM

WEATHER YOUR STORM

WEATHER YOUR STORM

WEATHER YOUR STORM

I did it.

I wrote it out.

I wrote out the stress, anxiety and fear around hurricane Irma's coming, storming through and then leaving Florida. Writing about it made me feel calm because as I wrote each poem, it took my mind away from what was happening, if only for a few minutes. Writing slowed down my mind and give me a chance to think - to prepare a plan B in case we needed it.

Now its your Turn.
Write it out.
Write (or draw pictures) about whatever is making you anxious or afraid.
What do you think is the solution?
Talk to someone (or a few people).
Ask for advise.
Don't keep your worries to yourself.
You conquer things by identifying them and making a plan to deal with them.
Start by identifying them.
Start here.
Its your turn.
Start writing.
Take care.

Sherra

Book Series: Living Lively

An imprint of SGS Publishing
www.LookItsTheBook.com

JOURNAL

Weather Your Storm

www.ingramcontent.com/pod-product-compliance
Lightning Source LLC
Chambersburg PA
CBHW020423010526
44118CB00010B/392